Harry Carter
— Cornish Smuggler —

An autobiography
1749-1£

Tor Mark Pres

Cover picture reproduced by permission of
Mary Evans Picture Library.

Other books in this series

Antiquities of the Cornish Countryside
China Clay
The Cornish Fishing Industry
Cornish Folklore
Cornish Legends
Cornish Mining — Underground
Cornish Mining — At Surface
Cornish Recipes
Cornwall's Early Lifeboats
Cornwall's Engine Houses
Cornwall's Railways
Customs and Superstitions from Cornish Folklore
Demons, Ghosts and Spectres in Cornish Folklore
Exploring Cornwall with your car
Historic Houses, Castles and Gardens
Introducing Cornwall
Shipwrecks Around Land's End
Shipwrecks Around the Lizard
Shipwrecks Around Mounts Bay
Shipwrecks — St Ives to Bude
The Story of Cornwall
The Story of Cornwall's Churches
The Story of the Cornish Language
The Story of St Ives
Surfing South-West
Tales of the Cornish Fishermen
Tales of the Cornish Miners
Tales of the Cornish Smugglers
Tales of the Cornish Wreckers
Truro Cathedral
Twelve Walks on the Lizard
Victorian Cornwall

This edition first published 1991 by Tor Mark Press,
Islington Wharf, Penryn, Cornwall TR10 8AT
© 1991 Tor Mark Press
ISBN 0-85025-327-6

Printed in Great Britain by Swannack Brown & Co Ltd, Hull

Introduction

Autobiographies of 'ordinary' people of the eighteenth century are not common; few indeed tell of lives as fascinating as that of Harry Carter, who was born in 1749 and wrote his autobiography sixty years later. The area where Carter spent his youth was on the north shore of Mounts Bay, on the coast between Marazion and Porthleven, and the centre of smuggling was in Prussia Cove.

When Carter was a child, Cornwall west of Helston was a remote land, with scarcely any roads passable by wheeled vehicles. Even in Penzance, the sight of a cart or carriage caused much comment. Packhorses, or more commonly mules, wound their way along inland paths now forgotten. A living could be made, with hardship fom the sea by fishing, with much difficulty from the barren land by farming, with risk both physical and financial by mining, or by 'fair trading'. Most of the smugglers combined their activities with a legal trade, and the receivers on land included people of all classes – squires and rectors as well as tin-streamers.

Cornishmen knew smuggling was against the law, but they believed it was not immoral; it was the law which was wrong! And in this they were not alone; Adam Smith, begetter of Tory economic thinking, declared a smuggler was 'a person who, though no doubt highly blamable for violating the laws of his country, is frequently incapable of violating those of natural justice and who would have been in every respect an excellent citizen had not the laws of his country made that a crime which Nature never meant to be so'.

Reading Harry Carter's story, one cannot but suspect that behind his family there are powerful influences at work. The exchange of prisoners which brings him back from France in 1778 and the grant of his commission to go privateering are otherwise very surprising. The ease with which he lives openly at home when outlawed shows how the whole countryside was united against the law; it was said of the excise officers that 'they wore fog spectacles with banknote shades'. When the price of a cargo of brandy in Roscoff was £1500, and the resale price in Britain £3000, it is hardly surprising that rich landowners (who were also the local magistrates), farmers and merchants were willing investors who could also be relied on for protection if things went wrong, nor that the prevention service might sometimes be persuaded to look the wrong way.

The smugglers were often considered pillars of their community. Even the Collector of Customs at Penzance described one Richard Pentreath of Mousehole as 'an honest man in all his dealings though a notorious smuggler'. When some 'free trade goods' belonging to Harry Carter's brother John were seized by the customs officers, and he went by night to retrieve them, the officers said to one another, 'We know John Carter has been here, and we know it because he is an upright man, and has taken nothing away which was not his own.' Strong ethical standards, especially standards of honest dealing between traders, were quite normal and were backed by the tenets of Methodism. No hypocrisy was involved, because these men did not accept their trade was immoral – although Wesley himself had preached against it.

For the historian, Carter's experiences in early Methodist communities and his internment in revolutionary France at the height of the Terror are of great significance, but for most readers his activity as a smuggler will be of more interest. This edition consequently omits a substantial part of the religious aspect, particularly in America, although leaving sufficient to give the reader an impression of the writer's state of mind. It has also been, for the most part, transcribed into modern spelling: although the original spelling gives a flavour of Cornish speech of the period, for example 'yest' for 'just', it stands in the way of an appreciation of Harry Carter's remarkably direct style. A few characteristic examples have been left, for example 'caled' for 'called', 'car' for 'carry' and 'likewayse' for 'likewise'.

The manuscript was handed down in the Carter family and was first published in 1894, with an introduction and notes by John B Cornish, under the title *The Autobiography of a Cornish Smuggler*, a reprint of this edition was published by D Bradford Barton in 1971. Readers who want to study the text in detail will find the Barton edition is still fairly easily available.

As it have been imprest upon my mind for several years to take a memorandum of the kind dealings of God to my soul, in particular these last two or three years, I have been persuaded by several of my friends, in particular Mr Wormsley and Geo. Carter. I have thought in general it would be so weak that no person of sense would ever publish it to the world, notwithstanding, this morning being 20 of Dec. 1809, I have taken up my pen, and may the Lord bring past things to my remembrance just as they are, and if published to the world, may the Lord make it a blessing to every soul that read and hear it for Christ's sake, amen, amen.

I have made several remarks at different times in years past of some particular things of my experience for my own amusement, then thinking for no person ever to see it but myself only; and as I have made a general rule more or less for several years to have had fixed times to sit in silence to trace my whole life from 8 or 9 years of age, in particular more so since I have tasted the goodness of God, most particular things that I have passed through seems to be tolerable familiar to me.

I was born in the year of 1749 in Pengersick, in the parish of Breage, in the County of Cornwall. My mother had ten children, eight sons and two daughters, eight of whom lived to maturity. My father was a miner – likewayse rented a little farm of about £12 per year – who was a hard labouring man, and brought up his family in what we caled [called: local pronunciation] decent poverty. My oldest and youngest brothers were brought up to good country scholars, but the rest of my brothers with myself, as soon as we was able, obliged to work in order to contribute a little to help to support a large family, so that I never was keept to school but only to read in what we caled then the great Book. As for our Religion, we were brought up like the rest of our neighbours, to say some prayers after we were in the bed, and go to Church on particular times as occasion sarv'd us. When I was about 8 or 9 years old, my brother Francis was about four years older than me. He joined the methodist society in Rudgeon, soon after found peace with God, and as him and me was most times sleeping and waking together he revealed himself unto me, told me the place and time he received the Comforter. I seeing such very great change upon him, as before he was a very active boy, I farmley believed the report. From that time I farmley believed that except I was born again I should in no case see the kingdom of God, so that convictions followed me sharp and often, sometimes constrained to weep bitterly. But alas! as I grew up they went fewer and fainter. About 9 or 10 years old went to work to stamps, and continued there until 15 or 16. I worked to bal, as I think, until I was about 17, and from thence went with my oldest brothers to Porthleah or the King's Cove afishing and smuggling, and I think about 18 or 19 times went at times, with Folkestone people and sometimes with Irish, as supercargo, whom we freighted. Before this time I learned to write, and so far so, that I would keep my own accounts.

I think I might have been about 25 when I went into a small sloop, about 16 or 18 tons, with two men beside myself, asmuggling, where I had very great success; and after a while I had a new sloop built for me, about 32 tons. My success was rather beyond common, and after a time we bought a small cutter of about 50 tons and about ten men. I sailed in her one year, and I suppose made more safe voyages than have been ever made since or before with any single person. So by this time I begun to think something of myself, convictions still following sharply at times. I always had a dislike to swearing, and made a law on board, if any of the sailors should swear, was poneshed. Nevertheless my intention was not pure; I had some byends in it, the bottom of it was only pride. I wanted to be noted to be something out of the common way of others, still I always had a dislike to hear others swearing. Well, then, I think I was counted what the world cales a good sort of man, good humoured, not proud, etc. But man is short sighted, who can discern spirits when the heart is deceitful above all thing and desperately wicked, oftentimes burning and boiling within a blaze of passion, though not to be seen without. Nevertheless in the meantime was capable to be guilty of outward sins the same as others of my companions, and often times, when went out on a party, crying and praying to keep me from a particular sin, was often the first that was guilty of committing it. Then conscience after staring me in the face, oh what a torment within I feelt. So I went on for many years sinning and repenting.

Well, then, in the course of these few years, as we card [carried: local pronunciation] a large trade with other vessels also, we gained a large sum of money, and being a speculating family was not satisfied with small things. Built a new cutter, about 197 tons, then one of the first in England; expecting to make all our fortunes in a hurry. I was in her at sea in Dec. 1777, made one voyage about Christmas. Returning to Guernsey light, sprung the bowsprit; was recommended from Guernsey to St Malo for a bowsprit and for the want of Customhouse papers and proper despatches was seized upon by the admiralty of the above place, where they unbent the sails, took them onshore, and confined us all on board with a guard of soldiers as prisoners, allowing two men to be on deck only at a time; likenwayse their orders was for no person to come alongside, no letters to pass or repass. But the commanding officer I soon got in his favour, that I conveyed letters onshore, and sent an express to Guernsey, likewayse to Roscoff, when there was soon certificates sent them to certify what I was, as they stopped me under the pretence of being a pirate; their pretence nevertheless was not altogether unreasonable, I having sixteen carriage guns on board and thirty-six men without any maritime pass, or anything to show for them.

I think it was on the 30 Jan. 1778, and I think the latter end of March there was an embargo laid on all English bottoms. They keept me onboard with all the people until I think the 1 May, when they took me onshore in order to examine me, and about four o'clock sent with a strong guard unto the Castle. This was a strange seeing unto me, the first prison I ever saw the inside of, the hearing of so many iron doors opening, etc. So I was put up to the last floor in the top of that very high Castle, in a criminal jail, where there were a little short dirty straw, etc.

So after looking round a little to see my new habitation, I asked of the jailor to send me a chair to sit on, and something to eat, as I took nothing for the day, then seeming to be in tolerable spirits; but as the jailor left me, hearing the rattling of the doors and the noise of the keys, I begun to reflect, where am I now? I shall surely never come out of this place whilst the war lasts, surely I shall die here, etc. I suppose in the course of an half hour heard the doors and keys as before for a long time before I saw any person, so in came a man with a chair, my bed, and a little soup, etc. Well, then, I sat myself down in the chair, looked at my dinner, etc., but then begun to weep bitterly. I had not lost only my liberty but the cutter also, which was my God. My liberty was gone, my honour, my property, my life, and my God, all was gone; and all the ten thousand pounds I expected to get privateering was gone, as there was a commission sent for me against the Americans before I left home. There I walked the dismal place bewailing my sad case. But in the space of about two hours two or three of my people were sent to join me, and before night I think about eighteen of us, small room full. Then we begun to sing and make a noise, so that some of my tears vanished away; hope of life sprung up, and as, the Franch was such flatterers in general, a very little hope for the cutter, etc. The remainder of the ship's company put in the town criminal jail.

We was all keept in prison until about the 20 or 21 day of the same month, when early in the morning were took out by a strong guard of soldiers, sent to Dinan prison of war, where we had then plenty of room. I suppose we were about six or seven of us that every evening joined to sing psalms in parts, etc. But this would not satisfy me, I know there was no Religion in this at all, but one night as I was asleep, as we lay on the floor side by side, I dreamed that I heard like the voice of an angel saying unto me, 'Except thou reform thy life, thou must totally be lost for ever'. There was something more that he said, but I cannot now remember it. When I awaked I was in a lake, sweat from head to foot, and all my body in a tremble. Nothing but fear and horror upon my mind. The next day I passed much to myself, very serious and sad, not one smile on my countenance, but keept it all to myself. Took great care to let no person know anything of the matter. Well, then, as Cain went to build a city in order to divert his mind, I begun to larn navigation, and so loosed my convictions little and little, that in the course of about a fortnight I could do the same as I formerly used to do. I think I was in prison about five or six weeks until my oldest brother John was brought to join me, as he come to St Malo just after I was stopped from Guernsey, with certificates from the Governor, etc., in order to try to liberate the cutter and me. Well, then, this almost so great trial as any, he being the head of the family, and thought the business must come to an end at home. We was kept both in prison until, I think, some time in August, and was sent on parole about forty miles in a town called Josselin. However, we was keeped in different places in the country until I think the latter end of Nov. in 1779, when we were private exchanged, by the order of the Lords of the Admiralty, in the room of two French gentlemen sent to France in our room. And then to come by the way of Ostend, being, as well I can remember, about five hundred miles. From thence came by the way of London, and arrived at home the 24 Dec. in the same year. We found the family all alive and well, but with the loss of the cutter, and the business not managed well at home, as my brother was then a prisoner, and wanting from home about two years, the family in a low state. Nevertheless, he being well respected with the Guarnsey marchants, was offered credit with many of them.

So went on again in freighting of large vessels, and had very good speed for some time. I went again in the little cutter I had before, about 50 tons. And after making two or three voyages to the King's Cove, went with a cargo on the coast of Wales. In order to smuggle it, went ashore to sell it. Left the cutter to anchor near the Mumbles, where an information was given to an armship called *The Three Brothers* that lay some distance from there. And about that time there had been some large privateers' cutters on that coast from Dunkirk, and had taken many prizes, manned and commanded chiefly with Irishmen. My cutter was represented to be one of them, namely, the *Black Prince*, mounting sixteen guns and sixty men. I had then in the cutter about six men and three beside myself onshore. When they saw the armship coming upon them, cut the cable and went to sea; and when the ship gave up the chase from the cutter, sent his boats onshore, took up the cutter's cable and anchor and found me onshore. I having left my commission on board, and had nothing to show who or what I was, took me on board the ship as a pirate, and after examining me in the cabin for two or three hours, detained me as a prisoner for twelve weeks until I was cleared by my friends at home through the Lords of the Admiralty. So after I was at home some time, riding about the country getting freights, collecting money for the company, etc. etc., we bought a cutter about 160 tons, nineteen guns. I went in her sometime asmuggling, and had great success. We had a new lugger built, which mounted twenty guns, and both went in company together from Guernsey, smuggling along the coast, so that by this time I begun to think something of myself again. Nevertheless convictions never left me long together. But in the course of this time, being exposed to more company and sailors of all descriptions, larned to swear at times. And once, after discharging our cargo, brought the both vessels to an anchor in Newlyn Road, when we had an express sent us from St Ives of a large cutter privateer from Dunkirk, called the *Black Prince*, had been on that coast and had taken many prizes, to go out in pursuit of her. It was not a very agreeable business; notwithstanding for fear to offend the collector, we put round the both vessels to St Ives Road, and after staying there two or three days, the same cutter hove in sight Christmas day in the morning. We not having our proper crews on board, collected a few men together, and went to sea in pursuit of him. Soon come up with him, so that after a running fight for three or four hours, as we, not being half manned, and the sea very big, the shots so uncertain, the lugger received a shot that was obliged to bear up, and in the course of less than an hour after I received a shot that card [carried] off my jib, and another in the hull, that we could hardly keep her free. So that we bore up after the lugger, not knowing what was the matter of her running away. We came up with her about five in the evening. Desired the Captain to quit her, but he, in hope to put her into Padstow, continued pumping and bailing until about six, when he hail'd me, saying, stand by him, he was going to quit her. So that they hoisted out their boat, but the sea being so big and the men being confused, filled her with water, so that they could not free her nomore. I got my boat out in the meantime, sent her alongside the lugger, so that some of the men jumped overboard, and my boat picked them up, and immediately the lugger went down. I hove to the cutter and laid her to, that she drifted right over the place that the lugger went down, so that some of the men got on board by virtue of ropes hove from the cutter, some got hold of the jib tack, and some picked up by the cutter's boat, so that we saved alive seventeen men and fourteen drowned. As Providence would have it was about the full of the moon, or certainly all must be lost. This was scene indeed. What cries! what screeches! what confusion was there! We stayed some little time there cruising about the place, but soon obliged to get the cutter under a double reefed trysail, a heavy gale of wind ensuing, and bore up for the Mumbles.

Now I am going to inform you of a little more of my pride and vanity, the spirit of truth had not as yet forgot to strive with me. Before we come up with the privateer, in expecting to come to an engagement, oh, what horror was upon my mind for fear of death, as I know I must come to judgment sure and certain. If I died, I should be lost for ever. Notwithstanding all this I made the greatest outward show of bravery, and, through pride and presumption, exposed myself to the greatest danger. I stood on the companion until the wad of enemies' shot flew in fire about me, and I suppose the wind of the shot struck me down on the deck as the shot took in the mainsail right in line with me. One of my officers helped me up, thought I was wounded, and he would not suffer me to go there nomore. This was a great salvation, and that of God, and not the only one; for all so many hundreds of shot have flyed around me, I never received so much as a blemish in one of my fingers; but I can remember for many years before this, whenever I expected to come to an engagement, I was always struck with horror of mind, knowing I was not fit to die; and since I have tasted of the goodness of God, I have thought that the greatest hero in the Army or Navy, as long as the spirit of Truth continue to strive with them, even Anson, is struck with the like feelings; and if ever I hear of a coward, I know this is the cause of it.

In the year of 19th April, 1786, I was married to Elizabeth Flindel, of Helford, in the parish of Manaccan, and on April 19, in 1787, she bore me a daughter, who was called after her mother's name, and I think it was about middle of Nov. I went in a lugger, asmuggling, about 140 tons, mounting sixteen carriage guns. After making one voyage at home to the King's Cove I got freight for Cawsand, and as I depended on them people to look out if there were any danger, according to their promise, came into the Bay, and after some time spoke with a boat from the above place, saying it was a clear coast, there was no danger to bring the vessel up to anchor, and we should have boats enough out to discharge all the cargo immediately. So that I brought the vessel to anchor, leaving the jib with the trysail and mizen set, and begun to make ready, opening the hatches etc., when I saw two boats rowing up from the shore. I said to the pilot, 'There is two boats acoming.' He answered, 'They are our boats coming to take the goods out.' Soon after a boat come alongside. 'Do you know these is two man-o'-war's boats?' We immediately cut the cable, and before the lugger gathered headway [they] were right under the starn. They immediately cut off the mizen sheet, and with a musket shot off the trysal tack and boarded us over the starn. My people having some muskets, dropped them down and went below. I knowing nothing of that, thought that all would stand by me. I begun to engage them as well as I could without anything in my hands, as they took us in surprise so suddenly, I having my great coat on buttoned about me, I seeing none of my people, only one man at the helm; and when they saw no person to oppose them, turned upon me with their broad swords, and begun to beat away upon my head. I found the blows very heavy – crushed me down to the deck – and as I never loosed my senses, rambled forward. They still pursued me, beating and pushing me, so that I fell down on the deck on a small raft just out of their way. I suppose I might have been there about a quarter of an hour, until they had secured my people below, and after found me laying on the deck. One of them said. 'Here is one of the poor fellows dead.' Another made answer, 'Put the man below.' He answered again, saying, 'What use is it to put a dead man below?' and so on. About this time the vessel struck aground, the wind being about East S.E. very hard, right on the shore. So there I laid very quiet for near the space of two hours, hearing their discourse as they walked by me, the night being very dark on the 30 Jan. 1788. When some of them saw me lying there, said, 'Here lays one of the fellows dead,' one of them answered as before, 'Put him below.' Another said, 'The man is dead.'

The commanding officer gave orders for a lantern and candle to be brought, so they took up one of my legs, as I was lying upon my belly; he let it go, and it fell as dead down on the deck. He likewayse put his hand up under my clothes, between my shirt and my skin, and then examined my head, and so concluded, saying, 'The man is so warm now as he was two hours back, but his head is all to atoms.' I have thought hundreds of times since what a miracle it was I neither sneezed, coughed, nor drew breath that they perceived in all this time, I suppose not less than ten or fifteen minutes. The water being ebbing, the vessel making a great heel towards the shore, so that in the course of a very little time after, as their two boats was made fast alongside, one of them broke adrift. Immediately there was orders given to man the other boat in order to fetch her; so that when I saw them in the state of confusion, their guard broken, I thought it was my time to make my escape, so I crept on my belly on the deck, and got over a large raft just before the mainmast, close by one of the men's heels, as he was standing there handing the trysail. When I got over the lee-side I thought I should be able to swim on shore in a stroke or two. I took hold of the burtins of the mast, and as I was lifting myself over the side, I was taken with the cramp in one of my thighs. So then I thought I should be drowned, but still willing to risk it, so that I let myself over the side very easily by a rope into the water, fearing my enemies would hear me and then let go. As I was very near the shore, I thought to swim onshore in the course of a stroke or two, as I used to swim so well, but soon found out my mistake. I was sinking almost like a stone, and hauling astarn in deeper water, when I gave up all hopes of life, and begun to swallow some water. I found a rope under my breast, so that I had not lost all my senses. I hauled upon it, and soon found one end fast to the side just where I went overboard, which gave me a little hope of life. So that when I got there, could not tell which was best, to call to the man-of-war's men to take me in, or to stay there and die, for my life and strength was almost exhausted; but whilst I was thinking of this, touched bottom with my feet. Hope then sprung up, and I soon found another rope, leading towards the head of the vessel in shoaler water, so that I veered upon one and hauled upon the other that brought me under the bowsprit, and then at times, upon the send of a sea, my feet was almost dry. I thought then I would soon be out of their way. Left go the rope, but as soon as I attempted to run, fell down, and as I fell, looking round about me, saw three men standing close by me. I know they were the man-of-war's men seeing for the boat, so I lyed there quiet for some little time, and then creeped upon my belly I suppose about the distance of fifty yards; and as the ground was scuddy, some flat rock mixed with channels of sand, I saw before me a channel of white sand, and for fear to be seen creeping over it, which would take some time, not knowing there was anything the matter with me, made the second attempt to run, and fell in the same manner as before. My brother Charles being there, looking out for the vessel, desired some of Cawsand men to go down to see if they could pick up any of the men dead or alive, not expecting ever to see me any more, almost sure I was ither shot or drowned. One of them saw me fall, ran to my assistance, and taking hold of me under the arms says, 'Who are you?' So as I thought him to be an enemy, made no answer. He said, 'Fear not, I am a friend; come with me.' And by that time forth was two more come, which took me under both arms, and the other pushed me in the back, and so dragged me up to the town. I suppose it might have been about the distance of the fifth part of a mile. My strength was almost exhausted; my breath, nay, my life, was almost gone. They took me into a room where there were seven or eight of Cawsand men and my brother Charles, and when he saw me, knew me by my great coat, and cryed with joy, 'This is my brother!' So then they immediately stripped off my wet clothes, and one of them pulled off his shirt from off him and put on me, sent for a doctor, and put me to bed. Well, then, I have thought many a time since what a wonder it was. The bone of my nose cut right in two, nothing but a bit of skin holding it, and two very large cuts in my head, that two or three pieces of my skull worked out afterwards; and after so long laying on the deck with that very cold weather, and being not altogether drowned, but almost, I think, I did not know I was wounded or lost any blood.

And now, my dear reader, I am going to show you the hardening nature of sin. When I was struggling in the water for life I gave up all hope, I was dead in my own mind; nevertheless my conscience was so dead asleep I thought nothing about Heaven or hell or judgement; and if I had died then I am sure I should have awakened amongst devils and damned spirits. See here this great salvation and that of the Lord. I have been very near drowned, I think, twice before this, and have been exposed to many dangers many a time in the course of time between the five years the lugger was lost in the North Channel and this time, privateering, smuggling etc., but I think conscience never so dead as now. I stayed there that night and the next evening took chaise. My brother and me, and the doctor came with us so far as Lostwithiel, and arrived at home the night after to brother Charles' house. I stayed there about six or seven days, until it was advertised in the papers, I think three hundred pounds for apprehending the Captain for three months from the date thereof, which sent us all of alarm. So I moved from there to a gentleman's house at Marazion. I think I stayed there about two or three weeks, and from thence moved to Acton Castle, as my brother John rented the farm, the family not being there then, so that the keys and care of the house were left to his charge, and after a few days removed to Marazion again, then afraid of the shaking of a leaf. I think I might have stayed at Marazion for the course of a fortnight, and then went to the Castle again. I used to half burn my coals by night in order that there should be no smoke seen in the daytime. In the course of about three months, after my wounds were nearly healed, I used to go at night to the King's Cove and there to drink grog, etc., with the Cove boys until the grey of the morning, convictions following me very sharp still at times. In my way home to my dreary lodgings, the larks flying up in the fields around me, warbling out their little beautiful notes, used to move me with envy, saying, 'These dear little birds answer the end they were sent in the world for, but me, the worst of all creatures that ever was made.' So that I have wished many a time I had been a toad, a serpent, or anything, so that I had no soul, for I know I must give an account for my conduct in this world. Likewayse there was a grey thrush that sang to me night and morning close to the house, which have preached to me many a sermon.

In the daytime I chiefly spent my time improving my learning on navigation, etc. I remember one Sabbath day, when I was at Marazion, I heard some people singing of hymns. I think they were Lady Huntingdon's people, when sincerely wished I had been one of them. I often thought there was very great beauty in religion, and when I have been with others laughing and ridiculing the methodists, wished I had been one of them, whom I thought best of them. See what hypocrite was here. I remember about a year before this I went with my wife to Caerlean preaching, on the Sunday afternoon, where I stood as near as I could by the door. When the word fastened upon my mind, saying, 'Thou art the man.' So that I was constrained to turn my face to the wall and weep bitterly, with promises to mend my life. But, alas! I had not gone perhaps an hundred yards from the house until I joined my old companions, so lost all my convictions. That was not the only time by many when I have set up resolutions in my own strength to serve the Lord, etc. Well, then, in the course of this time, whilst at this place, my wife would come to see me, and sometimes bring the child with her, and spend a day or two, so that I passed my time pleasantly whilst she was with me. I think it was in the latter end of August my wife was taken very poorly in consumption, being before of a delicate constitution, and was always obliged to come and go at night. I think it was in the beginning of Oct. in 1788 when I went to Helford to see her, in company with a servant man to brother John, one night, as she removed from her own house to be with her mother. I found her in a very weak state, and as I expected then soon to quit the country, I stayed with her about two or three hours, when we took our final farewell of each other, never expecting to see each other no more in time. Oh, what trying scene it was, to leave her in flood of tears. So I arrived home to my dreary solitude a little before day. I, before then, was greatly distressed for her soul, and through friends desired Uncle James Thomas to visit her, so he did often. I think it was about the 10 or 12 of the same month, when I was sitting upon a bench in one of the ground floors, bemoaning my sad estate, I began to say to myself, 'I have lost my liberty, my property; I have lost my wife also' – as she was the same as dead to me then – so I thought that if her life were spared, it mattered little to me if I was to go to the West or East Indies, so that I could only hear from her by letters, would leave me some comfort. But that was taken away also; so that when I was cut off from every comfort in this life, that I had not the least straw to lay hold of, I begun to see the emptiness and vanity of everything here below, and set up the resolution, God being my Helper, I will serve him the remnant of my days, so that I immediately fell to my knees and begun to say, 'Lord, have mercy upon me. Christ, have mercy upon me,' etc.; and at that time I could not say the Lord's Prayer without form, if any man would give me my liberty, being so long living without prayer. So, then, as before time I used to divert myself in the daytime in looking at the ships and boats in the bay, the men and cattle working in the fields etc., but now shut my eyes against them all; and if I had business in the daytime to go to the top of the house, was with my eyes shut. So I went on with the above prayer, sometimes in hope of mercy, othertimes lost almost all hope. Oct. 24, in 1788, sailed from Mounts Bay for Leghorn in the ship *George*, Capt. Dewen, master. Was put on board with a boat from the King's Cove, accompanied by brother John, and I think I was almost like a dead man; thought little or nothing concerning my wife or child, or anything in this world, but was earnestly crying for mercy. I had a little cabin to myself to lodge in, where there was only a single partition between me and the men, At first it was a great pain to me to hear them swearing, but after a little while took very little notice of it. I had some very good books to read with me, but they seem to be all locked up to me, as the natural man cannot desarn the things of the Spirit of God, for they are to be spiritually desarned. I remember sometimes reading, when I could not understand, I should be so peevish and fretful that I could heave the book overboard. Then, oh, what a torment in my poor soul I feeled. Then to think, surely the mercy of God is clean gone from me. Oh, what burthen my life was unto me. At them times I seldom prayed less in secret than twelve times a day and night, and when I could pray with a little liberty, I should be in hope of mercy, and at other times kneel down and groan without one word brought to my remembrance, then almost ready to give up all, saying, 'Surely there is no mercy for me; all my prayers is no use at all, God pays no respect unto them;' but still I dare not give up praying. I could look back afterward and see I was all prayer. So I think I arrived at Leghorn in the latter end of December, where I passed my Christmas. I think the first Sabbath after I came there the captain asked me to go on shore to church with him, as there was an English church and clergyman there. I gladly went. The minister being a good reader, I saw in his countenance much gravity and solemnity. I said to myself, 'Surely this is the man of God,' and thought I was highly favoured to hear him. The next Sunday I gladly went again, but on coming on board after the service was over, I was told that sacrament days he did not scruple to go to the plays and cards, etc., which poisoned my mind so with prejudice, I never went nomore. In the course of all this time I never meet with one person to give me one word of advice concerning my soul, but I laboured to keep myself to myself so much as possible, still reading and praying with all diligence. Well, then the captain got a freight there to go to Barcelona, to load with brandy for New York in America. I was very glad when I heard of it, as I heard that there was methodists there, in hope I should fall in with some of them to give me a word of instruction. So I think we sailed from Leghorn in the latter end of Jan. 1789. I remember on my passage there one day, scudding before the wind, very cold weather, and a very big sea, looking over the starn. I thought I should be very glad to be tied in a rope and towed after the ship for a fortnight, if that would get me into the favour of God. But, alas! I know all such works would not merit anything from God as salvation. I arrived at New York on the 19 April in '89, and about ten or twelve days before I arrived there, I was taken with a violent inflammation in one of my eyes, so I could see very little on that eye and the other much affected also. So after two or three days being there, there came a glazier on board to put in a pane of glass in the cabin windows. And as the captain and mate was not present, I thought it was my time to enquire out the methodists, and as shame always hunted me so much, I begun to ask him about the different persuasions of people there; at last I asked, 'Is there any of Mr Wesley's methodists here?' He answered, 'There is many.' I asked him, 'Do you know any of them?' He answered, 'Yes, many of them.' I asked, 'What sort of people are they?' thinking, if he gave them a bad character, to say no further. His answer, 'They are a good sort of people,' so then I asked him, 'Do you know the preacher?' He said, 'I do, and I go to hear him sometimes.' I said, 'Then I shall be obliged to you if you will send your little boy with me to show me the preacher's house.' So after he stared a little at me, said, 'If you will stay a little until I have done this job, I will ither go with you myself or git some person that shall.' So that encouraged me very much, set me in high spirits, and after a little further discourse, he told me his wife was a methodist, and soon after took me to his house, where the dear woman received me very kindly. And when she know I wanted to speak to the preacher, she asked me if I did belong to the connection in England. I answered, 'No, but I wants to speak to the preacher.' She said, 'Tonight is public meeting night. I will go with you a half hour sooner, when we shall find Mr Dickinson home.' So accordingly we went together, where we found the dear man and his wife in the kitchen, As soon as I looked at him, I said to myself, 'This is the man I wants to see; this is the man of God.' I said, 'Sir, I should be glad to speak a few words with you.' So as there was no persons present but his wife and the good woman that come with me, said, 'Say on.' I said, 'To yourself, if you please, sir.' So he took me into a small parlour and said, 'What do you want of me?' I said, 'Sir, I am an

Englishman, and belong to a ship in the harbour. I know I am a great sinner, and as I am informed you belongs to Mr Wesley's people, I want to know what I must do.' He looked at me and said, 'Do you think God would be just to send you to hell?' I was surprised at such a question, did not know what answer to make. Then he begun to say to this purpose, that Christ come to seek and to save that which was lost, etc. He likewayse asked me, 'Do you pray?' I said, 'Yes, a little.' 'Do you fast too?' said he. I said, 'No, sir.' So, after asking me a few more questions he said, 'There is a public prayer meeting here this evening, you may stay if you please.' So I thought he paid me a very great compliment. I thanked him, and when the time come, that dear woman took me to the meeting house and put me in a place to sit down. So after they had sung and prayed, the preacher gave an exhortation, and I thought all to me, so that I was a little comforted; and after the meeting was ended, the dear woman took me by the hand, as I was half blind, and led me home to her own house; and with the good glazier, her husband, led me on board, with a strict charge not to fail coming to see them tomorrow. So I gladly accepted of the invitation, and when I came there she had brought one of the class leaders and a good old woman to meet me, who gave me great encouragement to seek the Lord. My eye still getting worse, and as I could not get leeches as I used to do at home, applied to a doctor, and he cut the small blood-vessels of the apple of my eye, and so let the blood out. So as the ship was going to Baltimore to load, I thought if I went in her I should be in danger to lose the sight of one eye if not both, as both was much affected. So, then, I concluded to stay there, where I attended all the ordinance; some place to go to every night.

[At this point in the manuscript Captain Carter describes in much detail his spiritual troubles, and the ministrations of the Methodist preacher and congregation. He begins systematic fasting, and is in time convinced of his own conversion. Any reader interested in this record of early Methodism in America may refer to the edition published in 1971 by D Bradford Barton under the title *Autobiography of a Cornish Smuggler.*]

I think it was in the latter end of August when I received a letter from my mother-in-law concerning my wife's death. I soon begun to reason if she was gone happy or not, so that in the course of a few days after I used to go out by night, and looking up towards heaven, wishing and praying to see her vision, or to know by some means whether she was gone happy or not. And one night, before I went to bed, I prayed earnestly to the Lord if he would show me by dream or by vision. So that night I dreamed I was amongst serpents and vipers, and the worst of venemest beasts, that I had the hardest struggle to get clear of them, so when I awaked I was in a lake of sweat from head to foot. Then I thought I had not done according to the will of God. I continued in that state, with my harp hanged upon the willows, could not sing one note for a thousand worlds for all so much delight I took in it in times past, keep it all this time to myself, so that I got myself into such wilderness state that I could hardly tell if I was in the favour of God or not. But I think it was to the end about fourteen days I opened my mind to Mrs Snow, who said, 'By your own account your wife had good morals, and she had also the preachers and people to pray and instruct her; I have a good hope she is gone happy. Nevertheless, whether or not, you must leave that to God, it is a business you must have nothing at all to do with; and if you continue to go on in this way, I am in doubt as you are in danger to lose all your Religion.' So we kneeled down and she prayed for me, and immediately I went to a prayer meeting.

[Four months of religious experience have here been omitted for reasons of space.]

On 21 December went to a prayer meeting where I met Mr Hodgson providently, and after the meeting he asked me to go home to his house with him. I gladly embraced the opportunity, and after a little conversation by his fireside the Lord enabled me to believe in him for full salvation. I immediately told him, saying, 'Glory be to God, I do believe.' So after we sung and prayed, he said, 'You must go in the morning and tell your friends of what the Lord have done for you; this blessing may not be given for your sake only, but for others also.' So I parted with him, and went home, jumping, and leaping, and praising of God. And the next morning, according to his order, I went from house to house, and told the six or seven families that I was most particular acquainted with what the Lord had done for my soul, so that we rejoiced greatly together, they farmely believed the report. And I have thought many times since, as if I hard them say, 'Now we see God have no respect of persons. This poor ignorant Englishman have been here with us only a few months, have been justified and sanctified, and surely if this blessing is to be attained to, we will never rest until we receive it.' So that the preachers and people were all in alarm. In the course of a few days there were new prayer meetings set up upon almost every quarter of the town, so that in a very little time the Chapel would scarcely hold half of the people, and the Lord begun to pour a lot of his spirit upon the people in a wonderful manner – some crying for mercy, others standing up rejoicing and praising of God that they know their sins was forgiven them; likewayse others rejoicing, saying that God spake the second time, 'Be clean,' and cast out all their inbred sin; and oh, what a glorious work was there. I know one of my friends going home from a prayer meeting one night, about two or three o'clock in the morning, called to another friend's house, knocked him out of bed, and told him that God cleansed him from all unrighteousness. They both joined in prayer, and they wrasled with God until the other experienced the same blessing also. So that with the noise and brusel [bustle] of the people the world seemed as it were turned upside down. The Calvinists, Baptists, Universalists,

Quakers, with the people of the Establish Church, all seemed to rise up in arms against it. Some said the devil was amongst the methodists, some one thing, some another; but the work continued to go on in a glorious manner, so that in the course of about two or three months the society increased from about 260 to more than 500. It was then good times indeed, praise be to God. I have had the pleasure to see many revivals since, but I think I never saw greater heroes for the work than my dear friends in New York; and I think the people there then was something like the primitive Christians, going from house to house in fellowship one with another, declaring the wonderful works of God. Well, then, I am now going to return to myself. I think it was in the beginning of January, in 1790, when there was a meeting set up caled the 'Select Bands', meant for those that was sanctified, and those believers that was pressing hard after it might join if they pleased. So I think there was about twenty that perfess sanctification joined, and about ten more that was crying after it. I think that was a school indeed, to hear so many sensible men and women to stand up to tell of their experience from the beginning to the present, and I never was a greater wonder to myself than to be permitted amongst such people, as I was the youngest in the way and the most ignorant of them all. So I still continued in all the ordinances, using not less secret prayer than when I begun to seek the Lord, my soul most times in a blaze of prayer.

I think it was in about the middle of January when I went one morning to the preacher's house in company with Mr Cooper, where there was several of the leaders, consulting where they should hold prayer meetings, and how they should car them on. I went home to my lodgings, and seating by the fire I begun first to reason, saying, 'Everyone is employed, all have some thing to do excepting me, and I am good for nothing, no use to society, but as a dead dog in the way.

Well, then, as I was a long time in expectation to have remittance from home, my money being done, and being in debt about 38 shillings for my board, I said to my creditor, 'I have gave up all hope of having any money from home, I must begin to work about something, but what or where I know not. If I work in town the people will brand me for a deceiver, as I have said I have some property and sent home for some, so I fear it would much hurt the cause of Christ. I should be glad to have your advice in the case,' He answered, 'What you owes me is but a trifle, you need not go anywhere to work on my account. You are welcome to stay a month or two longer, perhaps your money will come; and if not, do not make yourself uneasy about it.' But, however, my friend Hodgson about that time went upon Long Island to live, so that I spoke to him for lodgings and went with him, thinking I should be out of the way for censure. So the 12 of June I car'd my little sea bed there, and laid it in one corner of his room as he had neither steed [bedstead] for me; so the next morning, being 13, went to work to a farmer about a mile and half from the little town where I lived, and was sent to the field to hoe Indian corn in company with a negro.

The work was very strange unto me, but soon after begun fell into discourse with him, and I rejoiced to hear he belonged to New York society. We worked the forenoon in the field together, where I was pleased and profited with his conversation; the afternoon being hard rain, we worked shifting of straw, etc., in the barn, when come the farmer, as I could not mow hay, etc., paid me my wages, and directed me in my way home to a cousin of his, whom I called upon, and he told me to come the next morning. Accordingly I did so, who sent me in a field to do the same work, when about seven or eight o'clock I was joined with a man to work with me, who was part owner of the field. I worked until breakfast time, when I was called in to breakfast. I could eat nothing, but drink a little milk, the same to dinner. The man that worked with me, as he could do much more work than me, desired me not to work too hard, but by three or four o'clock the blood was running between my fingers, and my body so weak, almost ready to drop down. The man that was with me asked me no questions concerning who or what was, but a little before we left work went to a public house and brought me a little rum and water, and desired me to drink again and again. I gladly took a very little of it, and should have taken more, but I thought, as he know me to be a methodist, he did it in order to trap me; but I saw after the man had no such desire, so I gladly received it with thankfulness both to God and him. So I went home rambling, with a tired body, as one that was much intoxicated. The next morning went to the same place again, but wore gloves to hide my bleeding hands; and as their hours was from about sun rising, and stop a little to breakfast and dinner, and work until sun set, and as my body was wasted and weakened before with much fasting and abstinence, and had hardly dirtied my finger scarcely for nearly twenty years before, my body was almost ready to crush under the burden. Oh, what a change was this indeed! And as I used before to pray not less than twelve times in a day in secret, I had no opportunity at that time but a few minutes before I went to work, and find a little house or some bye corner to breakfast and dinner; and when I got home in the evening, where the family was almost ready to go to bed. But I can really say, to the glory of God, I never was so happy in all my life as I was at that time. So I stayed there two or three days to finish that job, and after put in a field to work to myself some distance from the house, and furder from my home, where my employer told me, 'You may lodge here if you will.' I gladly accepted the offer, and the first night I was took into a room in one end of the farm house and showed my bed, where there was an old negro woman, and a little black boy with her. I looked at my bed, the room, and my company, and I think I never saw a meaner bed in all the course of my life. Stripped off my clothes and turned in, in full expectation that they were going to sleep with me, as I saw no other bed or place for them. But whilst I was thinking of this, I saw there in one corner of the room a little ladder, where they both went up together. I was there, I think, three or four days in that field to myself, and I think it was the second day, about eleven o'clock, I stood in the field and leaned upon my hoe, and could not tell whether I should drop down under my burthen or stand any longer, the sun almost over my head, the wind very little, and took hardly anything to sustain nature. And I worked harder than perhaps I was required to, and that for two reasons – the one for fear that they should know I was a broken gentleman, and if known, I should not have work to do. The other, I must do justice unto my employer. Whilst I was thus at a stand, calling to the Lord for help, I saw a light shone brighter then the light of the sun, that filled me with such faith and love, I went on again like a giant refreshed with new wine, praising and blessing of God. Oh, what happy times I had every moment. After I had done the field, he had no work more for me, so I returned home and got work a day or two in a place. I keept all what I feeled to myself, no murmuring, no complaining; but when my dear friends in New York come to hear of it, they agreed together to contribute to my maintenance, and take me off from there, and sent me word to be home one day, as they were coming to see me. Accordingly the day came, when six or seven women come according to promise, and after some conversation opened their business, but in a very feeling manner. I thanked them, and said, 'I surely am not too good to work; I have read of some that have worked for their own bread that I am unworthy to wipe their shoes or snuff their candle.' So we passed the afternoon together in singing and praying. I saw them to the boat, where they made me promise not to fail to come to see them every Sunday, and, if possible, Saturday night.

After three or four days, working a day in a place, I went to work with a farmer near the place I worked before, where I went to hoe Indian corn with five or six negro slaves. They behaved unto me very civil indeed, desired me not to work too hard; and as the poorest workman amongst them could far outdo me and do my best, but one or other always helped me on, so that I kept close up with them. I was, as well as I can remember, with them six or seven days, and that time sleeped in a hay loft. My suffering was not all over as yet; I could eat very little, and in the morning, when I went to work, almost so sore and so tired as in the evening; and I could hardly say I could sleep at all, at times just forget myself only. All this time neither master nor any man ever asked me who or what I was, they only know I was an Englishman. They all treated me very civilly, and when they had done with me they would ask me my demands. My answer was, 'What you please'; so they always gave me the same as another common labourer. About this time I was asked to go with a mason to repair a mill dam; it was to be repaired with turf, and I had a small flat bottom boat to carry the turf across the pool. So I went with him upon this conditions, if I could do the work, to give me what he pleased. I expected at first he was to be always with me, but just showed me my work and left me to myself, only some times come to see me, once in the course of two or three days. I then lodged and boarded myself to friend Hodgson's. The place was in a bottom, in mirey ground, and the weather very hot, that the sweat would run over me in large drops, as if any person was heaving water upon me. I think I went to work about sun rising in the morning, I suppose about five o'clock, stop about half an hour to breakfast, only an hour to dinner, and then work until sun set, I suppose about seven. My breakfast and dinner was a piece of bread I car'd with me, and I went to a farm house for a little milk. When my employer come to see me, he would most times bring with him a little rum and a cup, and as there was a well close by, 'Come,' said he, 'rest yourself a little; let us go and have a drink together.' What a change indeed was worked upon me; before time, when I was, as it were, a gentleman, I could not touch a dram before dinner upon any account. But then how glad and thankful I was to receive it. But after the first fortnight or three weeks my bones was become a little more hardened, my sufferings was not altogether so much, and I have thought many a times when my sufferings was to the greatest, that if it was the will of Providence I would gladly continue in the same all the days of my life. So every Sabbath day I went to New York to see my friends in the morning and return back again in the evening.

I think it was in the later end of July when Mr Dawson, one of them English men I before mentioned that came from the County of Durham, came over and informed me that if I would go home there was a vessel that would be ready in the course of a week's time, and he was going to England. I thanked him and went to New York, and asked the advice of my friends. They all, as the voice of one man, said, 'Surely this is the Lord's doing; go, the Lord will be with you. We believe that it will not be in the power of man to hurt you, but you must not think it strange if you receive strong trials from the Captain.' The Captain was an Englishman that come there from the West Indies, and had been in town for, I suppose, six or seven weeks; a man that did profess Religion, and did at times stand up in public as a preacher, but of Calvinist principles. And as I know him before, I went and asked him for a passage, then fully believing it was my duty, and I thought I could trust the Lord with my both soul and body. So he was quite agreeable, and then, as I was not acquainted with the man, opened all my mind unto him, notwithstanding for all the hints I had concerning him before. So he asked me if I was a navigator, and if I could work, etc. I answered I had my quadrant and books with me. So I agreed with him to be landed in Mounts Bay, or close to the East of the Lizard Point, and then returned back to Long Island, and told my employer I was going home. He desired me to stay a few days longer with him to finish the job, to which I consented. And I think about the 3 or 4 of August, when we settled our accounts, he paid me very handsomely. I returned to New York. I paid off all my debts and bought myself several little seafaring clothes for the voyage, and I think I had four pence in coppers left. Well, then, here was a change in deed – from such hard labour to ease again. So I stayed there with my dear friends, going from house to house as before. I think I was always rejoicing and praising of God, and still using the same self-denial by abstaining from food as before time, and not only then, but also when I was to my hardest labour. I stayed there until the 13 August, when took breakfast with my old and first friends the glazier, and after breakfast he took a dollar out of his pocket and said, 'I insist on you to accept of it.' I thanked him, and I took it, so went on board, and that day got to anchor in Sandyhook, and the next morn sailed for England with a fair wind and fair weather. The vessel was a small sloop about 40 tons, bought by the captain then in New York, but the papers draw'd in the mate's name, under cover him being an American. The cargo was cooper's timber, and the whole crew was the Captain, mate, two boys, Mr Dawson, and myself. I keept one watch with the biggest boy, I suppose about 16 or 17 years old; and the mate keept the other watch with the other boy, I suppose about 13 or 14 years old. We was not more than a day or two at sea until Satan begun to rage and roar. The Captain set his face against me. Try my best I could do nothing to please him. He pretended to know all things, but hardly know anything of the sea or business. Then I thought of what I was told by my friends in New York, so that I was not the least disappointed. I acted in the capacity of steward and as cabin boy, to bring all things to his hand as a gentleman, and if there was anything short I stayed without it; so that I had plenty to do to try to please him, besides keep my regular watch on deck night and day. We had a fair wind until we came upon the banks of Newfoundland. Then the wind took us ahead and blow fresh for a little time. The vessel made some water upon one tack; he said, 'We will bear up for Boston.' I think, for all he was a professor of Religion, I never saw a man more afraid of his life in all my life. I thought that if we put in to Boston I never should fetch home in that vessel. I opposed him, and said, 'There is no danger, I will engage to keep the pump in my watch.' Mr Dawson said, 'I will keep it in the other,' though he know nothing of the sea. The mate then joined us, and amongst us all gained our point, so that soon after we had a fair wind again.

We had most times public prayers in the morning, sometimes Mr Dawson and sometimes him, but still continued with his face set against me, and poor Mr Dawson dare not speak one word in my favour, as he was full so much afraid of him as I was. And the two poor boys, I think in the hardness of my times it was never in my power to treat two dogs as he treated them. So one day, after we come in to soundings, I said, 'The Land's End bears so and so, it is time for you to alter your course if you land me there.' So as he pretended to keep a reckoning, he said to the contrary, but never let us see his journal, the mate and me, within two or three miles of each other, so that I thought he had no mind to land me in the Mounts Bay, according to promise, the weather being fair. Saw a sail, and as it was not the first time by many, said to me, as I had the helm, 'Bear down to speak with him.' I did so. He said, 'Keep her so and so.' I said, 'Sir if you keep her so, you never will speak with him.' He begun to belch out, 'What is that to thee? I say keep her so.' So as I had given up all hope of being landed there, I thought it was time to take a little courage. I left go the helm and said, 'Keep her so your self, if you please,' and I immediately went below and turned in in my cabin. In the course of a little time he came down and said some thing to me in a very surly manner. I answered, 'Sir, you have not behaved unto me as a man since I have been with you. I have answered every end I engaged with you for, and much more so, and now I see you are entirely off your word with me, as you know you was to land me in the Mounts Bay, or a little to the East of the Lizard.' He begun to bawl out, 'Thou dost profess the spirit of Christ, but thou hast the spirit of the devil,' and so on in a great rage, my poor friend Dawson present fearing and trembling but dare not speak one word; and I have thought that good man suffered during the voyage much more on my account than I did myself. So I did not render railing for railing, said nothing, or very little more. This was in the evening, and in the course of about half hour after, when he come to himself, he came to me and said in a very good humour, 'I should be glad if you would turn out and come on deck, I wants to speak with you.' So he took me forward on the bow out of sight and hearing of any person, and said something to this purpose: 'I hope you'll think nothing of all that is past, and I am going to tell you why I cannot be to my word with you to land you in the Mounts Bay. I sarved my time to a hatter in London, and as there was a brig there loaden with hats and other goods, I took her away under the pretence of being supercargo, unknown to the owners. I sold the vessel and cargo in the West Indies, bought the sloop you see me come to New York in, sold that sloop there, and bought what we are in at present. I told you and others I was bound to London, but I meant to go to Dunkirk and send to London for my wife. I mean to sell my cargo and then to return to New York again, for if I am known in any part of England I shall be apprehended and hanged. So now let me beg you to keep it a secret. And I have the favour likewayse, as you know there is no draft for the Channel on board, I knows nothing of the Channel, and the mate quite unacquainted, let me beg you to do your best to carry the vessel to Dunkirk.' I answered, 'I will do everything in my power, etc. This was the tenor of our discourse. So that when he had finished, I thought I was almost lost in wonder and astonishment. I thought my case was bad, but his ten thousand times worse. So I turned to work again with a willing mind, knowing nothing should happen unto me against the knowledge of God, neither without his permission, and I believed all things should work together for my good, and so went on my way, rejoicing and praising of God.

The weather still very fair and a fair wind. The next morning saw the Start Point, and so made the best of our way up Channel. When came a little to the west of Folkestone, Mr Dawson was put onshore, to go to London in order to fetch the captain's wife to him to Dunkirk, and soon after fell in with a fleet of West Indiamen, with several cutters and frigates, with their boats out, bring them to to press their men, as at that time there was a little quarrel between the Spanyards and English. We passed through them all with our American colours set, expecting to be brought to every moment; and as I was the only Englishman on board, the captain advised me to hide myself in the bread locker. But I thought, if they had come on board and found me, I must be gone; so I thought if it was the will of Providence that I should be pressed, let his will be done; and I thought if they should come on board and ask me if I was an Englishman, I should say nothing to the contrary. That if I was stationed on the tops, or anywhere else, God would be with me, and all things should work together for my good. The same day, about three or four o'clock, got close in to Calais, where we took a pilot for Dunkirk the same evening, on the 16 September in '90. And as we went up the harbour I saw in a brig's stern, I think, the 'Bettsy, Truro.' I thought if there was any place caled by that name out of Cornwall, but the next day, as the Captain and I was so great he could then not go onshore without me, nither eat nor drink without me, I was then with him as it were all and in all. It was a great change indeed, whether through fear or love I know not. So the next day I, as a compliment, asked him to go on board with me to see what the brig was. So it proved to be from Truro, from Petersburg loaden with hemp and iron, there wind bound, and bound to Daniel's Point [on the Fal] the first fair wind; and as I did not want to make myself known unto him as an Englishman, I thought I would let him know that I know some gentlemen at Falmouth, and after a little discourse some in Penzance; so after a while, he naming of one and another until he come home to our family, and added, 'Poor fellows, they have had a great many and very great misfortunes of late years. Harry, poor fellow, lost a valuable lugger, with a valuable cargo, and was obliged to leave his country, being taken with some man-a-war's boat. I saw him in Leghorn, dined and supped with him, and from there he went to America. I have not heard anything concerning him since; whether he is dead or alive, I know not, poor fellow.' So at last I said, 'I am the man, and I desire the favour of you to give me a passage home.' He stared like a man frightened, and said, 'I never saw such a change on any man in my life and I had no more knowledge of you no more than if I never saw you. Anything in my power I will gladly do for you. Do you want money, or anything else? You'll make free with me. I am sorry I cannot take you to sleep with me, as the cabin is full of hemp, etc. Be not afraid of being pressed, as all my men is protected, but you shall not be pressed unless they press me also.' Here I was lost in wonder, love and praise, seeing how I was presarved the day before from a man-of-war, and I looked upon this as if the Lord had worked a miracle to send the brig there as if it was on purpose for me.

The Captain used that trade for some time, but never put into any harbour in France before, but now struck upon a sand bank, and put in there to be repeared, as he had received some damage, etc. Well, then, I could but only wonder and adore the goodness of God, surely his paths is in the deep and his ways past finding out. So then I returned again to my little sloop. I stayed in Dunkirk eleven days, then sailed for England, arrived at Daniel's Point the 1 Oct. The same night, about nine o'clock, arrived home to Kenneggy to Br. Charles's. So I was received as one risen from the dead, as they know nothing of my coming home, neither had heard from me for about twelve months. So after a little I related what cause I had to come, and after I had settled my business I was minding to return to New York again. He said, 'I will send for our brothers in the morning, and praps we may find something otherwayse.' So early in the morning they come, and said 'If you go to America again we shall never see you more; we think you may stay at home in safety, there is no person will meddle with you, but we advise you first to go about this neighbourhood as public as you please, where you are well known, but shun the towns, and after a few days there will be no person take notice of you.'

I very gladly consented to what they said, this being on Saturday. First went to the King's Cove to see the Cove boys, and for all I was not more than about two years from them, not one of them know me until they heard me speak. The next morning being the sabbath, went to Trevean to preaching, where I had a blessed time indeed. After preaching I was surrounded with almost all the congregation. Every one glad to see me, but in particular the methodists, as they heard before that there was a change of mind passed upon me. This made me to wonder and adore the goodness of God unto me, as I did not expect to see any person when I came home but only my own family. This was a wonder indeed to think I was once more returned to my native country, amongst my own family, friends, and the people of God. Well, then, after attending the preaching and meetings a few times was desired to give out a hymn and speak in prayer, but at first I refused, as I did not exercise in that way before I come home, only at times I was sent to visit the sick with Father Cooper when he could not attend himself. So I refused, but after suffered great pain of mind, so that at last I took up the cross with much fear and trembling, and immediately went about like a town crier, telling the people what the Lord had done for my soul.

See what a change was here taken place; a little while before labouring in the fields with the poor negroes, and used like a slave, and looked upon with contempt on the greatest part of my passage home; so now I had nothing to do with the world, all things was provided for me, so that in a little time the congregation begin to increase greatly, and prayer meetings set on in many different places; so as far as I can remember, in the course of eight or nine weeks there was a great number of men, women and children converted. Our meeting seem to be all in confusion, some praying, some singing, some crying, some praising and blessing of God. We have stayed in the house some times from twelve until three o'clock in the morning. My heart at that time, with every power of my soul, was fully engaged in the work; one time in particular, I trust I shall never forget it, in prayer in the after meeting, I think Mr Watkins was the preacher, whether in the body or out of the body I could hardly tell. It was just the same as it was in New York, and car'd on in the same mannner. At the first some of the old members would not owned it to be of God, as it was so much out of the common way, whilst many others put their shoulders to do the work, and, praise be to God, about this time I do remember my soul through mercy was got just in the same tune as it was in New York. I declared at that time to several old members concerning my thoughts. Some would give me great encouragement, whilst other would try to drive me back.

Well, then, I was not confined to Trevean house only, but I went about all through the country. But no place where I was asked where the housen was not full of people, and some would not contain all the people. Surely I was a wonder to myself, and in general I found great freedom to speak to the people in my simple way. I remember once I went about eight or nine miles from home, and as I came to the door where I was expected, a young man came out and said, 'Are you Captain Harry Carter?' I answered, 'My name is Henry Carter.' He said, 'We have been expecting of you, for it is given out for you to preach to-night.' When I heard of the name preach, I was struck with such fear and trembling, I could not tell whether it was best to return home again or stay there. So I went in, and the good man received me very kindly, and when the time came took me to the chapel, where it was so full the people could hardly stand. Some that know nothing of preaching called it preaching, but I never presumed to take a text, but laid a little foundation as a text in disguise, so that I had room to ramble. But it was not for what I could say only that the housen was so full of people, but it was like the Jews of old, came not to see Jesus only, but Lazreth also. Where I was not known before, they heard of me, and they believed that there was a great change upon me. I think the people believed I was really what I professed to be, but many times after I had been speaking, so dejected in my own mind, wishing that I may stand up no more, for it was seldom a day passed but what I had doubts whether I was cal'd or not, and I was much afraid to run before I was sent. Well, then, still the work of God continued to go on in Trevean society, and lively meetings all through this neighbourhood.

I think it was in February in 1791, or a little before, when the work in Trevean begun in some degree to cease, but still blessed times; and I think it was in the later end of March or the beginning of April I was sent for by a great man of this neighbourhood, he wanted to speak with me. Accordingly I went, and the business was as follows – saying, 'I was in Helston a such a day in company with three gentlemen' (mentioned their names); 'they all ware black coats. Looking out through the window, a methodist preacher went up street. One said,

"There is a methodist preacher." Another answered, "I wonder how Harry Carter goes about so public a preaching and Law against him; I wonder how he is not aprended and taken." So I sent for you, as I fear they are brewing of mischief against you.' 'Well, sir,' said I, 'what do you think I am best to do?' He said, 'I know they cannot hurt you no further, than if you are taken you may suffer a long time in prison, and it may cost you a good deal of money, etc. I think you are better, to prevent danger, to return to America again.' This was the tenor of his advice, and added, 'If you go there I will give you, as I think he called it, a lett of recomendation from Lord _____, which, I think, may be very useful to you, or anything else in my power shall not be wanting.' And as the gent was well acquainted with our family, I dined with him, and he brought me about a mile in my way home, so I parted with him, fully determining in my own mind to soon see my dear friends in New York again. So I told my brothers what the news was, and that I was meaning to take the gent's advice. They answered, 'If you go to America we shall see you no more. We are meaning to car on a little trade in Roscoff in the brandy and gin way, and if you will go there you'll be as safe there as in America; likewayse, we shall pay you for your commission, and you car on a little business for yourself, if you please.' So that with prayer and supplication I made my request known unto God. I still continued to walk in the same rigorous self denial as before, abstaining from food, etc. Well, then, with much fear and trembling I concluded to go. The greatest trial I had about going, I know there was no religious people there, and some times in fears I should be led away into the world again. I know I was going on slippery ground, but, glory be to God, I know his grace was sufficient for me. So at the 19 of April, in '91, I sailed in an open boat from the King's Cove, in company with a merchant that had business there, so that after fifteen hours' passage arrived there very safe, still in the same frame of mind. I lodged at a public house, I think, two days, and as the merchant had business to Morlaix, desired me to go with him, where I stayed there about ten or twelve days, and returned again back to Roscoff. I keept myself to myself as much as possible. Well, then, I went to private lodgings and ate and drunk to myself; and as I had no business to do, I was almost all the time to myself day and night, still walking in the same self denial as first. I would not allow myself but four hours in bed, so continued, as well as I think, for six or seven days, but I found I had not sleep enough, as about noon I have fallen asleep upon the book, so I added a little longer time.

Well, then, I did not pray in secret less than I did before, I suppose never less than ten times in a day, and in fore and afternoon walked a little out of town in so solitary place as I could find, out of sight of all men. In general I went on the cleavs [cliffs] where no eye saw me, and there sing, that I may be heard for I suppose a mile distance, and pass, I think, about two hours and half fore noon and after noon in reading, praying, singing, and then return home. I passed almost all my time to myself; in my going out and coming in I went the byest roads, because I wanted to see no person; and if I meet any person in the way, it was a great cross to me to enter in to any conversation more than just the time of the day, for fear to obstruct my communion with God.

Well, then, I went on still in this way until I think about the beginning of August, when I went on with a little business in the shop way, and about the same time Captain B. came there, an old acquaintance of mine, being the first Captain I sailed with, a man of what we calls good morals. I meet him one Sabbath morning as I was walking out, and after a little conversation I said, 'This is a poor place for the public worship of God; if I was at home now I should be at Trevean preaching.' He answered, 'Why don't you stand up here and say something to the people?' So as I thought he was making game of me, I answered, 'Who will hear me?' He said, 'I will hear you, and I suppose most of the Englishmen in town.' So the next Sabbath morning met with him again on nearly the same ground. He repeated unto me nearly the same thing again, saying, 'All the English in town will gladly hear you,' or to that purpose. So then I thought he was in earnest, and I left him with much fear and trembling, and immediately went to ask counsel from the mouth of the Lord, so that spent the remainder of that fore noon in pray and supplication, and for fear I should run before I was sent, I set this as a mark, that after dinner I would go on the pier, and if I met first such a man, who was master of one of the vessels that was there, I should propose the matter unto him, and if agreeable, I should surely think it to be the will of God concerning me. So about one o'clock I rose up from my knees and went on the pier, and the first man I met with was the very same man, so with much fear and trembling I opened the business unto him of what Captain B. and I was talking of. He readily replied, 'I'll come, and I will tell all the people of it, I suppose they will all come.' So him and me proposed the time of meeting, I think it was four o'clock. Well, then, according to the time proposed, the same afternoon, in came Captain B. with I suppose about twenty or thirty, I suppose nearly all the Englishmen in the town, took off their hats, and seat themselves down, so that I begun to tremble and sweat, I could scarcely hold the hymn book in both hands. Gave out a verse, and begun to sing myself, and praise be to God, before I sung the second verse I found life coming, and before I went to prayer the cross was all gone, so that I found very great liberty in prayer; so that when I rose from my knees I was surprised to see so many hard hearts to their knees, so that I found much courage to go on in my poor simple way.

[Several passages have been omitted in which Captain Carter describes the prayer meetings he organises for visiting Cornish sailors – most of them doubtless purchasing brandy from him. He confesses to many spiritual problems, but never doubts the morality of the smuggler's trade.]

So I continued for eight or nine months every night when there was Englishmen there. I think it was in the beginning of the month of May '92, when three of my brother's children come to life with me, Fra, Henry, and Joanna Carter, and staid with me until the beginning of Sept, when I was like a hermit to myself as before.

Well, then, about the later end of Nov. I got a passage to come home not only to see my family friends, but my spiritual friends also. I can still see, glory be to God, I was still hungring and thirsting after him. I thought before I come home, if I could be permitted to come into preaching housen doors, I should be very happy, but praise be to God, I had rather the right hand of fellowship given me, the preaching houses full of people where I was expected, as before. I staid at home until 24 Dec; and as the war seemed to be near at hand between the Franch and English, inbarked at Coverack, onboard Captain R. John's. I had a blessed time in company with my dear friends there, two or three day wind bound. Arrived at Roscoff, Christmas day in the morning.

1 Jan 1793, oh, how short I comes in all things of what I would wish or ought to have been. There was no talk of war when I arrived there, all was quiet as when I left the place. I found my house, etc., just as I left it. I was then to myself as before, I went home like a hermit or a king blessing and praising of God. I continued to walk in the same selfdenial. I sent off most of my goods to Guernsey, sold some there, and kept some, what the law would allow me to bring home, as I was promised that a vessel should be sent to bring me home. So I think Feb 2 there was an embargo laid on all English vessels, and war declared between the both Kingdoms. I think it was in the latter end of March when I was sent to Morlaix as a prisoner, not close confined, but to appear every morning to the town house to sign my name. I was there nine or ten days, when I was ordered back to Roscoff again. Things at that time looked very gloomy, but glory be to God, I was not the least afraid of all the lions in France. I could trust both soul and body in the hands of my Redeemer, no murmuring, no complaining, the language of my heart was continually, 'Good is the will of the Lord, may thy will be done.' I stayed in Roscoff nine or ten days, when I was ordered again to Morlaix in company with Mr and Mrs McCulloch and Mr Clansie. I think in the beginning of May was sent back again to Roscoff, Mr M. and Mr C. in Roscoff the same time, where we was all obliged to go to the town house every day to sign our names. So continued until the beginning of August, when we got a passport in order to come home. In the course of this time, whilst in Morlaix, the same as at Roscoff, went to private lodgings. Walking still in the same rigorous selfdenial, etc. So as there was no other way for us to come home, Mr McCulloch bought a small vessel, about 40 tons, and bout the seven of eight hauled the vessel out in the Saddle Rock Road, and got all things on board ready for sea, when there was orders from the town house with a corvette's armed boat, ordered us in to the pier again. And this was

Providence indeed. Our whole crew consist as follows: Mr McCulloch was a gentleman merchant, lived in that town many years before, a man of good property, etc.; Mrs McCulloch, two sons, one a man, the other about twelve years old, one daughter, a young lady about eighteen or twenty years old, one servant man, two servant maidens, Mr Clansie, and myself, ten in number in all. And we concluded before, that the old gentleman and me was all the sailors, there was not one of the other eight that in no case could help themselves. The four females was sent onshore to Mr M.'s house, all the rest of us keept on board with a guard of soldiers for three days and three nights, the wind blowing very hard tho' fair. This vessel was condemned for sea for some time before, so that in the course of three days we had time to overhaul her, and I think I may safely say that there was scores of graving pieces in her not bigger than a man's hand; some of the timbers so rotten, that one might pick them off with one's fingers, the sails, masts, etc., in the like state. We had hard rain some part of that three days, where we was so wet below nearly as upon deck. The old gentleman have told me many times since, saying it was Providence prevented us from sailing, had we sailed then we should all be no more. You may be ready to ask, Why did we expose ourselves to so much danger? I answer, 'This was the third passport, and all contradicted [cancelled], and glad to get out of the mouths of the lions, as there was no other way.' So we was all sent on shore to Mr M.'s house with a guard of soldiers to be keept at the door, and the 15 of August, 1793, all marched to St Paul's [St Pol-de-Léon] with a guard of soldiers. I lodged and boarded in the house with Mr and Mrs M., where I had a good room and bed to sleep in, and a large garden to walk in.

I stayed there until the 12 or 13 September, 1793, when some officers came, sent by the town house; so after they examined us for money and papers, took us to the Town House, and after they measured our height, and asked us many foolish questions, took us to a prison caled the 'Retreat', in the same town. We arrived there a little after night, were all of us showed our apartment to lodge in. I had a nice little room to myself like a king. Here was another change, but a happy one, the language of my heart was, 'Good is the will of the Lord, may Thy will be done.' Nor could I help singing that night aloud when I went into bed. We all had our provision sent from the house we lodged before, and after four or five days passed, we was joined by several French gent. and ladies, and in about fourteen or fifteen days there was two armed horsemen sent in the prison to take Mr and Mrs M. from us, no person knowing where they were to be sent, but supposed they were to be sent to a small uninhabited island, a little off Brest harbour, and there to be starved to death. Oh, what tears and cries was there with their little family and many others. It was seldom I could shed tears, then I did plenty, and after dried up my tears and cheered myself up, and then went to his room, where I found him alone packing up his clothes, etc. I sat myself down in silence, I suppose for about ten minutes without one word; whether him or me spoke first, I know not, but he said in his usual pleasant way to this purpose, 'I fear not what man can do unto me. I can trust in Providence and not be afraid,' which set my heart all on fire with love; I could give them both up unto God, surely believing I should see them again. The remainder of the day was a solemn day unto me indeed, but a day of mourning through the whole house; after this there did seldom a day pass but what some gentleman and ladies was brought to join us, and in the beginning of Nov 1793 the lady I boarded with and some of her family was brought to us.

I used set times for reading, praying, walking, and thinking, as I did before when I was at liberty, and keept almost all the time to myself; I went to bed about ten or half past, and got up as soon as I could see daylight in the morning; and as the weather begun to alter, just to run in the garden about half hour in the fore noon, and the same in the after noon. At first people thought I was ither a natural fool or else mad; but my friend Clansie gave them an account of what kind of being I was. About this time I had word brought me, that all my goods I left in Roscoff was condemned and sold, I suppose they might have been to the amount of £40. I rejoiced with great joy when I heard of it, saying the Lord's will be done, knowing all things should work together for good. It appears clearly to me since that my will was wholly swallowed up in the will of God; I think I was then surely so dead to this world as ever I shall be. Well, then, as the people begin to increase more and more every day, Mr Clansie came with me in my little room. At first it was a great cross to me, but soon after, the oftener I saw him the better, far better I liked him, he acted like a father, a brother, my tutor, my servant. Glory be to God for such dear friends. He was a young gentleman merchant, a man of great natural abilities, and I suppose brought up in the first schools in Christendom. I knew his father and him from a child before, but was little acquainted with him before we became prisoners together, and I have thought many times since that there was not in the whole world two such men as Mr M. and he. About the 3 or 4 of Dec 1793 a guard of soldiers came into the prison and took with them my dear friend C., Mr T. McCulloch, with a great number of French gentlemen and ladies, so there was none of my family left, but Miss M., her dear little brother, and the two servant maidens. I think such a scene as that I never saw in all my life. I suppose there was not one dry face in all the house, either with men or women. There was not one person that know where they were to be sent to, but supposed they were all to be sent upon the same Island with Mr and Mrs M., and there to be starved to death. This was a day of mourning and lamentation indeed. I do not know that I shed one tear, tho' it was a solemn day with me, still the language of my heart was, 'Good is the will of the Lord, may the Lord's will be done.' But the trial was so great, the same as tearing the flesh from the bones.

About the 6 Dec 1793, when a guard of soldiers came to the prison, and took away I suppose between thirty and forty prisoners, and me one of them, where to go we knew not; but Providence interfered, and worked upon a French gentleman's mind, so that he took Miss McCulloch and her little brother, with the two maidens, to his own house, so that they all had liberty to walk the town when they pleased. This was the cause of great joy and gladness unto me. There was a few horses brought for the old and infirm to ride – two, which one was put in my hands, and ordered to ride it, with a charge to keep it to myself. We had about twelve French miles to go, so we arrived to Morlaix just after night, where, to my agreable surprise, found dear C., Mr T.M., and some gentlemen of Roscoff, whom I know before. We rejoiced greatly together, and then they gave an account of Mr and Mrs McCulloch; they was put from St Paul's to a town caled Landerneau, about twenty miles from St Paul's, in to a criminal gaol, where the first night had nothing to lie on but a little short dirty straw, and without one farding of money with them, and not one person in the town that they were acquainted with, but in the morning was visited with some gentlemen and ladies, who supplied them with a bed, and brought them provision. So we rejoiced greatly together in telling and hearing. Here as a blessed change again to me, to once more to be with my dear family at home again. This place we was now in was a gentleman's house, all the family thrust out and put into other prisons, and this house was made a prison of. The house was not large, but it was full of people below and aloft. I slept in one room, where there was fourteen beds, and there could not find the least corner to retire to myself but a little house. At that time it was very cold, but I did not mind that. I could not stay there long to a time, disturbed with one or other, as there was sixty or seventy prisoners there. I had not one farding of money, not nither of our family, but the law or rule was, by the order of the Convention, for the rich to maintain the poor. So I think I was maintained by the public for two days, when my friend C. got credit for himself and me, from a tavern close by. What a great change this was again, all the day long in nothing but a discord and noise. What a mercy it was I was not drawed away by the multitude to do evil. I can see now at this moment how I improved my time, how precious every moment was, I had always my book in my pocket ready to hand if I could find any place to seat, and sometimes, when I could find no place to seat, stand to read. All the people very civil to me, and in the beginning many of them introduced their conversation; but I did not find it profitable, it served to block the mind from prayer. Tho' I could understand and speak French on most common subjects, I soon gave them to think I know little or nothing, so by that means I saved myself from a great deal of empty chatchat, so by that means pass almost whole days, some times without speaking very little.

25 Dec, or Christmas day, 1793, Mr T.M. and Mr S. was taken from us, and out to a town caled Carhaix about thirty miles from Morlaix, and there they joined Mr and Mrs McCulloch; all the rest of us was

moved to another gent. house a few doors off, where we had more room, etc., Mr C, and me still left together, The first thing I always looked for first was a place to go in secret, and my friend C. would always look out for a place for himself and me to sleep in. I found a nice little place in the garret, with some old mats and other things I so enclosed, that it would just hold me to my knees, with my feet out of sight, where I might stay so long as I pleased, and no person disturb me. This was a blessed change again. I slept in a room with ten or twelve gentlemen, went to bed at ten o'clock, got up in the morning at five, spent an hour to myself, and at six went down stairs, and sat by the fire with the old men that guarded the house. To read, etc., until about half past seven or eight, when I should retire to my little garret until nine, when I should come down, make my bed, and run or walk in a large room until ten, and then retire again to my garret until one o'clock, when I was caled to dinner. After dinner, about two, I retired to my garret and stay there until half past three, come down and run in the room until four, then retire, and stay there until about seven or eight, stay down about half hour, and then pass in the garret until ten, bed time.

There was a small window in the garret about a foor square, without glass, but a leaf to shut and open, so that in the daytime could see to read by it, but at night I seat without any light, the days nearly the same length as they are in England. This garret was very cold indeed to the body, so that my hands was swollen very large with chilblains, sitting so many hours in the cold without fire.

Jan 1794, about the beginning of the year, Mr C. got me to sleep with him in his little room and one French gent. This was again a comfortable change; there we was together again, like to great kings. About the latter end of this month, I was desired by C. to speak to about twenty women caled nuns, being prisoners in the same house. I went with fear and trembling. They received me in a very pleasant manner, drew a chear, asked me to seat down. One of them, an old lady, the mother Confessor, asked me, was I ever baptised. I answered, 'Yes.' 'In what manner?' I answered, 'I was marked with the sign of the Cross in the name of the Father, and of the Son, and of the Holy Ghost.' I saw some thing very pleasant upon all their countenance, as it was the same way they themselves was baptised. They asked me a number of many fullish questions, that I was obliged to muster all the little French I could rise, as I could understand and speak anything about the common things of this life far better than the spiritual things, having no person to converse with about spiritual things. However, they kept me with them I suppose about half hour, still asking me questions, but at last asked me to kiss the Cross. I refused. They tried me again and again. I told them I could not, I dare not do it. So at last took my leave of them, and so came off rejoicing like a king. They are a loving people, and the nicest women I ever saw in France. I doubt not but many of them lives according to the light that is given them. They petted me very much, and told my friend afterward that if he could prevail upon me to turn to their Religion, I should be a good man. They thought I was earnestly crying for mercy, but was an entire strainger to the way of mercy. They always looked upon me afterward with the love of pity, and some of them was fond to converse with me. I think it was the 11 or 12 of Feb '94, I seat apart to prayer and fasting on a particular occasion for thirty hours without eating or drinking. At the 19 and 20 of the same month, I seat apart in prayer and fasting to ask of the Lord several favours for self and friends, with thanks for past mercies, forty-eight hours without eating and drinking. Oh, what a blessed time I had. I could not keep all this a secret from my friend, so he took me to reason several times, saying, 'You'll destroy the body,' and would entice me like a child to eat, and always took the pains to call me to dinner. So I thought it was reason what he said, and I thought I was going to too great extremes, so I thought for the time to come I would go without breakfast and supper as usual, and fast for thirty hours once month, for the time to come. I did not know then at that time I was thankful or humble, but even now, I know I was as less than nothing in the sight of God and all men. I know I was unworthy of the floor I walked on, and vilest of the vile in my own eyes. I never saw my short comings more clearer than I did in them days. Oh, how often I was crying out against my dryness and laziness of soul, my littleness of love etc. Sometimes, when I heard the clock strike, I used to rejoice, saying, 'Lord, one hour nearer to Eternity,' the same time mourn before God I did not spend it more to his glory. I think every moment of time was far more precious than fine gold. About this time there was numbers of gentlemen and ladies taken away to Brest that I personally know, and their heads chopped off with the gulenteen with a very little notice. I don't know I ever had a doubt of my own life, but I have had many of Mr M., and thought many times, should he be condemned to die, I would gladly die in his stead if Providence would have it. I knew he had much enemies, and why, because he was a liberal man and a man of power, and did do much good, and them he did do most good to was his greatest enemies, and it was such men as him in general suffered most. As for me, I thought I should never be found wanting with any person in the world. I know my child at home would be taken care of, so it was a matter of very little difference to me where the body was left, knowing I had a house not made with hands, eternal in the Heavens. I stayed there until the 15 June, 1794, when the house was cleared of all the prisoners, and then put to a convent a little out of Town, that was made a prison, caled the Calemaleets [Carmelites?], where there was about 270 men and women, the house very full of people. We arrived there about nine in the morning, and as Mr C. and me was shifting about the house seeing for a place, standing in the room talking together, he was taken with a fit and fell as dead in my arms. Soon others came to my assistance, and took him out in the yard as dead. It was very seldom that I shed tears, but then I did plentifully, as I was in mind he was no more; but the language of my heart was still may thy will be done; come life or death, take life and all away, good is the will of the Lord. But praised be the Lord for ever, in the course of an hour he revived, and was put to bed, so that in the course of some time after he recovered. In the garden I seat myself under a tree and thought of Hagar's words, 'Thou, God, seest me.' I had a sweet time there until I was disturbed by two young men that came to seat by me with a great merriment and ladies, and soon after the Lord provided a place for me under the stairs. It was a large stone stairs going down to a underground cellar. In the daytime I could see a small glimering light, but never so light as to see to read. This was a blessed place again, where I was out of sight and hearing of all men. Mr C. got part of a room in the garret, with a young gent., whose name was Morrow. The first night I made my bed in the passage close by his door. Friend C. could not bear to see me there. The next morning him, with some young gent., got carpenter's tools and timber, turned to and divided the room into two, so took me in with him again, and there we was again together like two great kings. We could no longer have our food from the tavern, the distance being too far. The good lady that I lodged and boarded with in St Paul's was brought to the same prison, and a young gentleman with her, her brother son, to which she had dear C. and me with her to eat. She had her provision sent from her own house. Blessed be God for such dear Friends. In the course of two or three days I found my strength much failed me. I had more room to walk in than I had before, and long stairs to go up and down over. Mr C. discovered it, and took me again to reason, saying, 'You are of the earth, and the body must be helped with things of the earth; if you continue so, you'll hurt yourself, and if you do not feel any ill effects now you surely will if you lives until you are old.' I thought it was quite reason that he preached to me. I thought I was going too far with it, and that Satan had some hand in it; so after he watched me like a child, and if I was not present at the time of meals, he would come and fetch me, and I must go with him, he would not be denied. Praise be to God that I ever saw his face, he was always more mindful of me than he was of himself; so I continued to take breakfast for eight or nine days and then left it off again, and I only stayed without supper twice a week. This place was again a blessed change indeed. We had a large garden to walk in, from six in the morning until seven in the evening, I suppose not less than three acres of ground, with fine gravel walks in it and some apple trees, etc., so I was like a bird let out of a cage. I suppose I had not sung aloud to be heard with man for many months before. I was always surrounded with man, but then I used to go out with my book in my pocket, seat myself under a tree, and if I could not see any person, sing so loud, I suppose I might be heard for a mile off. Oh, how my soul would be delighted in the God of my salvation. I remember one day, as I was seating under a tree, three or four ladies came to me, and asked me to sing. I begged to be excused. They asked me again and again, so as I was afraid to give an offence I sung two or three verses with a loud voice. They thanked me in a very pleasant manner, and went away quite pleased I think I spent my time to myself much the same as I did in Roscoff, before I was taken as a prisoner. I was always mindful of my little corner under the stairs. I went to bed at ten o'clock, and got up in the morning at four. All the people still full of friendship to me; but I keept myself still to myself as much as possible, without giving an offence. There was there amongst the whole number about sixty nuns, one of whom I conversed with more than all the rest; seldom miss a day, if she saw me, but what she would have something to say unto me. But I had not French enough to enter into any depth of Religion, but I never heard one sound of persuasion from her to turn to her Religion. Once I remember she asked me, saying, 'Carter, did you not feel yourself very sorry when you was first convinced of sin?' or something to the same purpose. I was struck with wonder where she got that from. I think I may safely say she was a burning and a shining light. She had small supplies from her father's house, and well she had it often as it was possible. It was always in her power to govern her own mind. Every day she would give almost all she had to the poor, or to any person she thought that wanted; lived almost entirely on bread and water herself. She have often told friend C., 'Do not leave Carter want any thing, but speak to me.' I have often thought that she would almost tear out her eyes to do me good, and I have often thought that she had not the least doubt but what I was built for a Catholic. I have thought then, the same as I think now, that if I am faithful until death, and she continued in the same way, that she and me, with many more that I saw there, shall meet at God's right hand, where we shall sing louder and sweeter that ever I sung in the garden. May the Lord grant it. She was so nice, beautiful a young lady as I think the sun could shine on; I suppose about 26 or 27 years old. Her father was a nobleman of a large income, her mother, a sister to the great, rich Bishop of St Paul's, and him, as I have heard, for all his income, could scarcely keep a good suit of clothes about him – it was busy all for the poor. I think she was the picture of humility in all her deportment. I could not help to admire her, as I was in the same house, or houses, for, as I think, nearly six months.

I think it was in the middle of Dec 1794, the good lady and her brother's son was removed from us and put to St Paul's, into the prison that I was first put in. It was a day of mourning and lamentation with her, indeed, to leave her two children behind her, and it was a time of trial to me likewayse, as she was nearly so natural as a mother.

About this time I had an account that Mr and Mrs McCulloch was liberated out of prison, and they and all their family were then at Mr Diot's, in Morlaix. It was a day of rejoicing to me, indeed, to think that the Lord was so gracious to bring us so near together again. And in the course of a few weeks they had liberty to come to see dear C., and me in prison. We surely had a happy meeting together, as we had not seen each other for about fifteen months; they received me as their own child, and I them as my father and mother.

About the 10 Jan 1795, Mr Diot sent for me to come to dine with him. I went with much fear and trembling, as it was ever a cross to me to be with my great superiors, and so in every place I moved at a solemn awe of the presence of God resting upon me with a fear to offend him. There I met with Mr and Mrs M., with all their loving family, and through the tender mercy of God, after all our trials and sufferings, being separated to nearly sixteen months from each other, escaped, through mercy, all the lions in France, not one hair of our heads diminished. We stayed there until evening, when Mr Diot said, 'I will in the course of a few days get you out of prison and you shall both come to live at my house.' We thanked him, wished good night, and arrived at home with our guard about seven. So the 23 Jan 1795, in the morning, we was both liberated. I went to Mr Diot's, Mr C. went with Mr Morrow in the same town. Still provision at that time very scarce to be had, the inhabitants of the town had all their provisions served out every day according to their family. Without we had money we should not be able to get board on any account. I was received into that family as a king, treated as if I had been a nobleman, and being the last stranger was placed at the head of the table, where I begged to be excused again and again, but could not prevail. But to the end of six or seven days I shifted to the other end, where I thought I was more in my place. I thought it then, as I have many times since, a piece of bread behind the kitchen door was more suitable for me. Praise be to God, here was a change indeed. I eat most times my three meals, then for fear to be noticed, I always eat sparingly. I think I can say I always rose up with a sharper appetite than I had when I sat down. I lodged in a large house to myself next door to Mr Diot's, where I had no person to disturb me day nor night. This was a blessed change again, it was just the place I would wish to be in. I was there about two or three weeks, when I saw some things wanting to be done about two vessels that was laid up before my door, belonging to Mr Diot. I spoke of it to Mr Peter Diot, and went to work, and when the season served, I washed the decks morning and evening; and as I had a chest of carpenter's tools in the same room with me, made boats' oars, rudders, painted names in the stern of the small boats, etc.; that I was mostly imployed all the week. But my work not hard, as I was my own master, and I did it all voluntary. And on the Sabbath day I went out of town every morning and afternoon when the weather was fair in some solitary place to read, pray, sing and think, as I did in other places.

I think it was about the middle of March 1795, Mr M. was taken sick with fever and agues, and in the beginning of May 1795 went away with all his family, leaving only the two maidens and me behind him. It was nearly about this time I went with about half a score men to put a boat of Mr Diot's in a large building that was before a tobacco manufactury in the shade, and after I had got the boat to the place I wanted, I went from the people to get a corner to myself to pray, and looking about I saw a large scales and weights close by me. I thought as no person saw me I would weigh myself, and all the weight my weight was 6 score and 15 pound. [135lb. Cornish people never used the 'stone' of 14lb.] I was set to wonder where all my weight was gone, as I did for many years before weigh 10 score [200lb.], and when I came home I tried on a waistcoat that I had not worn for several years before, and I found it too big for me, maybe upon the round nine inches, and I never know in all these years no not one single day of sickness. I think it was the 10 July, 1795, the Captain of a frigate that was taken, and Mr Morriss of the *Elazander* man-of-war, came to Morlaix in order to get a passage to England in a vessel, who dined and supped at Mr Diot's. They made very free with me all the same as if I was their equal, and one day, by a friend, desired me to call at their lodging, they wanted to speak with me. I went with fear and trembling, and the business was as follows. They said, 'Mr C., we have been talking about you, as you have been here so long a prisoner, wearing your old clothes out, your time passing away, earning nothing. We think you may go with us in safety. Put your clothes on board the evening before we sail, get on board in the night, you'll never be enquired after, nither found wanting.' I answered to this purpose: 'Gentlemen, I thank you kindly, but first you'll give me leave to inform you I was brought out of prison upon Mr Diot's interest, tho' he never signed any paper, nither gave his word that I should continue in the country. Notwithstanding that, in these critical times, if I was to go without his leave, he might be caled to account for it afterward. If you will be as good as to ask Mr Diot, and with his leave, I will gladly go with you.' They commended me very much, and said the first opportunity they would ask him, and I should know of them again. In the course of two or three days I waited on them again. Mr Morriss said to me, 'Well, Mr C., we have opend your case to Mr Diot. Mrs Diot said, take him along with you; he is a great fool to stop here so long as he have, I wonder how he have not gone long before now. But Mr D. said you was best to stay a little longer,' and added, 'Mr C., providence has preserved and provided for you in a merciful manner, so I would advise you to wait with patience, and you will be delivered in God's due time.' I thanked them and took my leave of them, wondering where that should come from, for it was the words of a spiritual man. I went in one of my solitary corners and there sung, and blessed and praised God. I can almost feel at this moment how happy and thankful I was, so well and contented to stay as to go; and if it was the will of God, I should stay there all my lifetime, still, good is the will of the Lord, may His will be done.

So I continued to my work about the boats and vessels as before, walking in the same self denial, until the 6 or 7 of August, 1795, when, unexpected, on Saturday received a letter from Mr McCulloch to meet him at St Paul's next Monday, that he had obtained a passport for himself, family and me to go to England, and Mr Clansie was then at Brest, who had then got a neutral ship to take us home. Well, then, this was a great as well as unexpected news, and many times before then thought that I should be very glad and thankful if ever I lived to see such change. But it answered the same effect as every other change I passed through, a fear I should meet with anything that should obstruct my communion with the Lord, and this is my meaning when you read of any case before, when I said I went in fear and trembling. So that on Monday morning I set out for St Paul's in company with Mrs Diot and her two little children and two servants riding in a coach, and me on horseback, where we arrived at St Paul's at ten in the morning, and there joined Mr and Mrs M. and their loving family. Stayed there until Tuesday morning with my dear old friend and Mother, Madam Esel le Pleary, and set out for Landerneau in company with the two maidens. We arrived at Landerneau about three in the afternoon. Wednesday morning breakfast with my two old friends, Mr and Madame Elel Renard, and old gent. and young lady, who was his daughter. We was many months prisoners together, but then all liberated, and they in their own house. Same morning took a boat, and at four in the afternoon arrived on board the ship in Brest harbour, where we met all the family together, the same ten of us that was stopped together through a miracle of mercy indeed, and not one hair of our heads diminished. Praise be to God, here was another change. This ship was formerly an English frigate, then under Danish colours, and the captain an Englishman. The first night I slept on the cabin floor covered with a great coat, then got a hammock amongst the sailors. And when more people came on board, I went between decks, being more quiet. I suppose the whole number of passengers was about fifty officers in the army and navy, where I never was in such hurry and noise yet, in all the course of my life, nither to sea nor land. I was always employed in reading, in cooking, tending my family to the table, etc. And there was a black boy, the servant to one of the officers, very ill most of the time, and no person to do the least thing for him but myself only. I had a quiet place between decks to lodge in and pray, so that no person disturbed me. I used the same self-denial as before. I have been often led to wonder many times since of the goodness of God, for all they were such wild, distracted, dissipated souls, I never had the least trial from one of them, nither one of the ship's company during the whole time. I could always bring any dish of meat from the cook to the cabin to my family, and no person set the least hand on me; or if one of the others did, they was ready almost to kill one the other; and the captain would trust me with the tea and sugar canister, but not one person else on board.

We lay in Brest Roade nine days wind bound, and then got a fair wind to the northward and westward, arrived at Falmouth 22 August 1795. Arrived onshore about three o'clock in the afternoon with much fear and trembling, where I meet with my dear little Bettsy, there staying with her aunt, Mrs Smythe, then between 8 and 9 years old. In the evening went to prayer meeting in the great Chapel. It is now brought into my remembrance as the ship lyed off Falmouth harbour, there was not boats enough to carry all the passengers and baggage at once, and I waited to the last with two more, stayed until another boat should come, the wind blowing fresh from the westward. The Captain grew very impatient, looking out for a boat, and at last said, 'I shall not wait only a few minutes longer, and take you with me.' One of these passengers was making such a noise, almost ready to jump overboard, for fear to be car'd up Channel. I said to him, 'Have a little patience, we shall have a boat in little time now,' He turned unto me in a very sulky manner, and said, 'Who is like you, you are always at home, you don't care where you are car'd.' I smiled, said nothing, but rejoiced within, and said to myself, 'You are saying the truth.' And I thought if it was the will of the Lord that I should be car'd to Copenhagen, that good is the will of the Lord. So in the course of a few minutes after saw a boat coming, and so all was well again. Well, then, I stayed that night at Falmouth, the next morning went to Penryn with my dear little Bettsey in my hand, to see Mr McCulloch and his loving family, who was then at Mrs Scot. The next morning, on Sunday, took a horse and arrived at Breage Church town about eleven o'clock, where I meet my dear brother Frank, then in his way to Church. As I first took him in surprise, at first I could hardly make him sensible I was his brother, being nearly two years without hearing whether I was dead or alive. But when he come to himself as it were, we rejoiced together with exceeding great joy indeed. We went to his house in Rinsey, and after dinner went to see brother John. We sent him word before I was coming. But he could hardly believe it, with the voice of, 'How can these things be?' But first looking out with his glass saw me yet a great way off. Ran to meet me, fell upon my neck, and said in language like this, 'This is my brother that was dead, but is alive again; he was lost, but is found.' We passed the afternoon with him, and in the evening went to Keneggy to see brother Charles, where we meet with many tears of joy, and afterwards returned to Rinsey in the evening, where we had all our conversation about Heavenly things, which was a treat indeed, after being so long silent on the subject.